WHOSE LIFE?! IS THIS ANYWAY?!
Making Your Life Your Story

Your Guided Workbook to Finding & Starting What You Want in Life While Enjoying the Process

KETURAH JENKINS

HARRIS Author Services

www.harrisauthorservices.com

All rights reserved. No part of this publication may be reproduced, stored in a retrieval system, distributed, or transmitted in any form or by any means, including photocopying, recording, or other electronic or mechanical methods, without the prior written permission of the author. For permission requests, write to the author using the methods below.

ISBN: 978-1-7327696-0-1

Copyright © 2018 by Keturah C. Jenkins

Web: www.YourLife-YourStory.net
Email: info@YourLife-YourStory.net
Phone/Text: 502-209-7623

Ordering Information:
Quantity sales. Special discounts are available on quantity purchases by corporations, associations, churches, and others. For details, contact the author using the means above.

For my husband Rodney (who was well worth the wait), and our children Eleanor (my Sweet Baby Girl) and Colin (my Bubby Bear).

Contents

Acknowledgements 1
Introduction 3
Feather Pen 5

Revision 1
   My Current Story 8
   Accomplishments 10
   Clean Up Time 12
   Next Stop, Your New Destination 14
   Distractions 16
   Out With the Old 18
   In With the New 20
   Keeping an Eye on Your Habits 22
   In Summary 24
   Making it Stick 26
   Congratulations 29

Revision 2
   Let's Get to Editing 33
   My Current Story 34
   Accomplishments 36
   Clean Up Time 38
   Next Stop, Your New Destination 40
   Distractions 42
   Out With the Old 44
   In With the New 46
   Keeping an Eye on Your Habits 48
   In Summary 50
   Making it Stick 52
   Congratulations 55

Revision 3
   Let's Get to Editing 59
   My Current Story 60
   Accomplishments 62
   Clean Up Time 64
   Next Stop, Your New Destination 66
   Distractions 68
   Out With the Old 70
   In With the New 72
   Keeping an Eye on Your Habits 74
   In Summary 76
   Making it Stick 78
   Congratulations 81

Revision 4
   Let's Get to Editing 85
   My Current Story 86
   Accomplishments 88
   Clean Up Time 90
   Next Stop, Your New Destination 92
   Distractions 94
   Out With the Old 96
   In With the New 98
   Keeping an Eye on Your Habits 100
   In Summary 102
   Making it Stick 104
   Congratulations 107

Notes 109

Acknowledgments

To Eva, for being the cheerleader in my life for the last 20+ years, and for believing that these thoughts were print-worthy. To Jordan, for bringing creativity to my words, and being my original illustrator. To Kaggia, for continually telling me I had a book inside of me waiting to get out. To Deon, for always challenging me to think bigger. To Kim, Jennifer and Lorian for your eye for detail. To David, for being my guide through the world of publishing. And finally, thank you to my mother for showing me the pure joy that can be found in a good book.

Introduction

You are a storyteller. With every word, action and look on your face, you're yelling your story into a big, red megaphone for all to hear. Not only do you tell your story every day, even more amazing (*and a little bit scary*) is the fact that your story is a living thing that is constantly changing. Every decision, thought and habit is writing, underlining and highlighting it. The way you go about your day actually determines if your current story will just get louder and louder or (*and here's the kicker*) if you're changing your story.

At the end of the day, the more effort you put into planning your story, the more likely it'll be that you'll actually like your story. But here's the thing: putting in that effort doesn't happen by accident, out of convenience, or because it "just fell into place." Yes, it does take effort. But that effort can be so enjoyable when you know it's getting you to the life you've only dreamed about.

Now, even with the best intentions, all great stories need revisions (*sometimes many*). These revisions don't mean you've failed – just that *you've* changed . . . or how you want to go about crafting your story has changed. In the words of the great Maya Angelou, "When you know better, do better." So give yourself the chance to look at your story from time to time, and it'll make sure you are still on the right track.

Within these pages, I invite you to grab your pen, (literally and figuratively) set aside some time, and create a space to start to plan your own epic story.

Remember: Every day you write your story. Why not make it a story that amazes you?

The Feather Pen...

I went old school and chose the feather pen to remind you that you are writing your life story every day. The pen because – the story – *is in your hands*, so you get to decide what is written next. Specifically, a feather pen because it reminds me of calligraphy, and if you have ever seen calligraphy (*or a pretty font in general*), you can tell that every line, every loop and every curve is beautifully and lovingly placed and never left to chance. It's clear the calligrapher has thought carefully about what he or she is writing and what stroke will come next. Now while this amount of planning does take time and some discipline, in the end, when you see the final product, you can see it's totally worth it. And that is how I want *you* to look at your life. Because when the final story is important and exciting enough to you, you will absolutely enjoy the journey.

My Current Story

Something to think about...

Imagine that you are the star of your own TV series. Before jumping into planning the wardrobe and shooting locations, think of how you would introduce yourself to the audience. What description about your personality, what matters most to you, your finances, family, or work life are important for the viewers to understand as they get to know you?

I want you to take these ideas and summarize them in the box marked "My Story." You can use bulleted phrases, or individual words; it's up to you. The most important idea is that it should represent where/what you are NOW – not what you want, what you imagine, or what you think your story should be.

Next, life is complicated. And so is your story. While it may be tempting to paint your story with a broad brush as either "great" or "horrible," this is hardly ever the case. You are likely basing these large strokes on either your general personality style or the week you just had vs. reality. Truly, your story has parts that you love, and other parts you wish would just disappear.

In the other two spaces provided, I want you to push yourself to put away that broad brush and look closely at the details to discover the "Favorite Parts" and the "Sticky Situations" of your story.

A few questions to get you started...
- When you think of your story, how large a role does career, money, relationships and family play in your story?
- What makes you most proud about where you are right now?
- The last time you truly enjoyed yourself, who were you with? What did you get out of it that you would love more of?
- What *doesn't* work for you about your story?
- What was the last situation that made you cry?

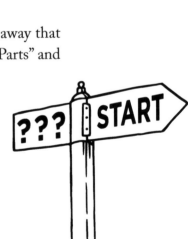

"Please think about your legacy because you're writing it every day."
—Gary Waynerchuck

My Current Story

My Story

Think where you currently are with things that are important to you (relationships, work, money, other). In phrases or single words, write your current story.

My FAVORITE Part

What makes you happy, proud or content about your story?

The STICKY Situation

What makes you sad, exhausted, or frustrated about your story?

Accomplishments

Something to think about...

Think about the next twelve months and think of four things that, once done, will make you "Ridiculously Proud". Consider this me highlighting and underlining the "Ridiculously Proud" part because it is important. These aren't goals you think you "should" have, what someone else thought would be a good idea for you, or someone else's expectations. This is something that deep down will make you jump for joy at putting them on the "Done" list.

So, with this excitement factor in mind, let's take a minute to talk about how to help you express this accomplishment. A common acronym used related to goals is SMART (*Specific, Measurable, Actionable, Realistic, Time Bound*). In this part, we will focus on Specific, Measurable, and Timebound when writing these accomplishments that will make you "Ridiculously Proud."

Start with **Specific** – clear/short (*example:* "I will be more financially responsible")

Add in **Measurable** – clearly know if you did it or not (*example:* "I will be more financially responsible by saving $500 to a separate emergency fund account.")

Tie it off with **Time Specific** – when you will be done (*example:* "I will be more financially responsible by saving $500 to a separate emergency fund by December 31st, 2019.")

Now you are ready to get going. Once you complete the list, look back over it. And if you aren't excited, you still have some thinking to do.

A few questions to get you started...

- What is your proudest accomplishment in life so far? What made it so memorable?
- What dream have you put off for too long?
- On a scale of one to ten, how would you rate your career, money, health, relationships? What accomplishment would make any of them a *fifteen*?
- What accomplishment have you thought, "There is no way I have the time or money to do that"?
- If someone were to write a news article about you in a year, what would you want it to say?

Accomplishments

Specific	Measurable	Time Specific
Clear/Short	Clearly know if you did it or not	When will you be done

On a scale of 1-10, how excited are you about this list? ☐

"What accomplishment(s) would make you RIDICULOUSLY PROUD?"
–Karen Eber

Clean Up Time

Something to think about...

Time to face up to those "Sticky Parts" of your story. No longer going the easy way of dodging them because either you don't have the energy to deal with them, or you are hoping they'll somehow magically disappear on their own. As you face them, also want you to avoid the temptation of just thinking about what makes them so sticky. Instead, focus on what you can actually do about them.

When thinking through how you can start to clean up these areas in your life, think about it in a few ways:

- **People** – Often the biggest hurdle is thinking you have to do it alone. You don't. There are people out there (that you already know or need to meet) that would enthusiastically help you. You just have to figure out who they are and then speak up and ask them for help.
- **Think/Say** – You have likely been telling yourself (and others) over and over again why this situation won't change. Here, write what NEW words/thoughts you will use to replace those old ones with that aren't helping you.
- **Get Moving** – What are the two things you can immediately do *this week* to begin cleaning up these situations?

A few questions to get you started...

- What would your life be like if these situations were gone?
- Who do you already know or would like to meet that could help you with the situation?
- Who can you ask for help?
- How do any of these "Sticky Situations" get in the way of the "Ridiculously Proud" accomplishments you listed?
- What have you been telling yourself about this situation? And how is that helping or hurting you getting past these "Sticky Situations"?

"The question isn't who is going to let me; it's who is going to stop me."
—Ayn Rand

Clean Up Time

List a few sticky parts from your original story and brainstorm "Solutions" you can use to change them.

STICKY SITUATIONS

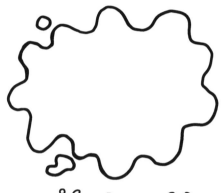
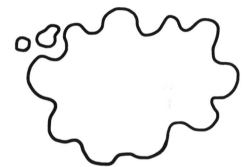

SOLUTIONS   SOLUTIONS   SOLUTIONS

People   People   People

Think/Say   Think/Say   Think/Say

Get Moving: List two things you can do THIS WEEK to start cleaning up these situations

Whose Life Is This Anyway?! Making Your Life Your Story

Next Stop, Your New Destination

Something to think about...

So now you have cozied up with your current story, looked at what you love and would love more of and gone deeper into what you want to change about it. Here you will consider the future, assuming that all of the "Sticky Situations" have been resolved and you have accomplished what you shared that would make you "Ridiculously Proud." Now, you will peek into the future to see what that new story is, with all of this in place.

Before you jump straight into writing, I want you to first sit back and imagine the *NEW* story in full color with surround sound. Make sure you are in a place where you can really use your imagination and think about what this new story would feel like, taste like, and be like to live in every day. When (and only when) you have that clear picture, down to what you'll be wearing (ok not that detailed, but you get the point), I want you to write it in this step.

IMPORTANT: While technically you are writing this step as a future goal, you will write it in the present tense AS IF IT IS ALREADY TRUE. Use language like "I am" instead of "I will be"; and use "I have" instead of "I would have." By writing it in the present tense, it will begin to be more real to you.

A few questions to get you started...

- If you could talk to yourself 10 years in the future, what would that version of you say?
- If you weren't concerned about what anyone else thought, what would be your perfect story?
- Stepping into this new story, what feelings are there?
- Think of someone you admire. What about their story makes you want to be around them?
- With the "Ridiculously Proud" accomplishments behind you, what additional accomplishments would you now be ready for?

Next Stop, your NEW Destination

My NEW Story

Describe the future assuming that all of the "Sticky Situations" have been resolved, and you have accomplished what you shared that would make you "Ridiculously Proud".

A Day in the Life

Describe a day in the life of your new story?

I'm PROUD...

What about this NEW story makes you most proud?

> "When writing the story of your life, don't let anyone else hold the pen." –Unknown

Whose Life Is This Anyway?! Making Your Life Your Story

Distractions

Something to think about...

With every amazing story, there are countless things lurking around every corner to distract you. The best way to stick to your plan is to already know they are coming and find ways to remind yourself of why your new story is more important than the distractions. While you can't plan for everything, you can spend time now thinking through some of the obvious ones, so you'll be ready.

Here is a good chance to look back at any of those "Sticky Situations" to see if they are getting in the way of your new story, and what you will do about them when they show up.

Hint: They are likely to be some things that are already standing in between you and your new story by sucking up your time but not getting you anywhere closer to your goals.

Another Hint: People/situations can be distractions.

A few questions to get you started...

- Think of the last time you felt yourself fully *in the zone*. What was it about your environment that helped you focus?
- How does the way you spend your time each day line up to the priorities you have for your life?
- The last time you sat down to accomplish a goal, what stopped you or slowed you down?
- How much time do you spend each day on social media or watching TV? Are you comfortable with the answer?
- When distractions come up, how will you show that you are committed to your goals?

"Starve your distractions feed your focus."
–Unknown

Distractions

List five distractions that are likely coming your way to throw you off your story.

1
2
3
4
5

How will you remind yourself that your story is more important than the distractions above?

Out With the Old

Something to think about...

Habits are wonderful things – until they get in the way of your story! Just like clothes, sometimes you outgrow your habits too. But instead of getting rid of them, you keep trying to stuff your life into them, even though they aren't comfortable and no longer make you look good. Now, think through your current habits and find those that no longer work for your new story. In addition to the habit, write out what it is about that habit that doesn't line up with the new story you came up with.

Hint: Thoughts can be habits too.

Current Habit	→	**How it Doesn't Line up to my New Story**
Eating out every day for lunch	→	That money could be used to build up my savings account.
Thinking that "I'm not creative"	→	Stops me from trying new things.
Too much time on my phone	→	Takes away time from the development of my new business.

A few questions to get you started...

- What habits do you have that have added to or helped create the "Sticky Situations" in your life?
- What habits have you had over the last five years that haven't changed, even though your life has changed?
- What habits have you been "meaning to," "thinking about" or "trying" to change?
- When you think about people around you, what habits have you picked up from them that don't line up with your new story?
- What current habit is the largest barrier to you moving into your new story?

Out With the Old...

Standing between me and my new story

What HABITS have to go away?

 How does this old habit get in the way of your new story?

> "If you want something new, you have to stop doing something old." –Peter Drucker

In With the New

Something to think about...

Things happen, and stories change because you actually do something different, not because you think about changing them, would like to change them, or consider changing them. Hands down, the best way to bring your new story to life is by creating habits that line up with the story. Every day you are either reinforcing an old habit or creating a new habit. Period. There is no neutral. While you are "thinking about" or "maybe starting" the new habit, you are highlighting, underlining, and becoming more comfortable in your current habit.

Go back and refresh yourself on your new story. Take the time to fully remember not only what that new story looks like on you, but what it feels like, and what a day in the life of that story would be like. Then come back and write down three or four new habits that you will do daily, weekly, or monthly which will get you to start living this story today. As you think about these habits, make sure they are measurable. Here are a few examples:

Goal (not easy to measure)	Habit (easy to measure)
Be healthier	→ Go to the gym 3 times a week
Save more money	→ Add $25 per paycheck to my savings account
Spend less time watching TV	→ Watch 2 hours (or less) of TV a day

Keep it to three or four because tackling too many new habits at once can be overwhelming and **then you give up**. Also, tackling too few habits will make it impossible to see how you are getting closer to your story, and **then you give up** (*see the theme here?*). So, stick to three or four to get some progress. Remember, in writing your story there will be many chances for revision, so don't feel like you need to change everything at once. What is important is what you can do **consistently**.

A few questions to get you started...

- What is that habit you have been "thinking about" starting for a while that lines up to your new story?
- When you think through what a day in the life of your new story would look like, what do you see yourself doing every day?
- What habits do you admire in others that line up with your story?
- With the bad habits you committed to stopping now gone, what new habits do you have space for?
- What is the one habit that would make you most proud of your progress?

In With the NEW...

Write a few habits that you will start doing daily/weekly/monthly/etc. to make your new story real:

Goal	New Habit	How Often?

"Successful people are simply those with successful habits." –Brian Tracy

Keeping an Eye on Your Habits

Something to think about...

Now that you have zeroed in on the new habits that will help bring your story to life, let's talk about how you will see if you are actually practicing them. Unfortunately, just asking yourself won't work because memory (*not just yours, but everyone's*) is unreliable. All people (*you included*) tend to flavor the answer with what they *would like to believe* about themselves. This either leads to giving more credit than is deserved or being a harsher judge than necessary. Here we just want to be accurate, for better or worse, so we can understand if the change is actually working (*Yeah!*) or if a revision is needed (*Aw! But that's ok too*).

Since we can't rely on your faulty memory, in this step you will think through (*and set up*) ways that you plan to track those new habits. This is your chance to be creative. You don't only want to track them, but you want to track them in a way that gets you excited to do it and stay consistent.

Some inspiration to get you started...

- Do a web search for "Habit Trackers," and you will get an abundance of ideas, everything from the simple to the beautifully artistic. Find a few that get you excited.

- Write a simple checklist of your new habits and keep it clearly visible (*think refrigerator, bathroom sink, above your desk, screen saver on your phone*) of your new habits. Physically check them off as you practice the habit.

- Re-live grade school and creatively decorate one index card for each habit. Then hang them somewhere you will see them often throughout the day.

- Get a journal specifically for writing down a few lines at the end of every day, and grade yourself on how you are doing against your new habits.

- Find someone to partner with on the goal/habit so you both can help keep each other on track.

Keeping an Eye on Your Habits

"A goal without a plan is just a wish." —Antoine de Saint-Exupéry

Get creative on how you will keep your new habits front and center, and how you can tell if you actually are doing them.

New Habit	How will you keep track if you did it or not?	Have you created the tracker?
		☐ yes
		☐ yes
		☐ yes
		☐ yes

In Summary

Something to think about...

Now comes the time to begin to wrap up your new story with a lovely big bow. It's time to summarize your new story in such a neon-colored way that when you're tempted to slip back into old habits or need convincing why the effort will be worth it in the end, you have something short and sweet to help snap you back. Think of this as the shorthand representation of your new story.

Here's another opportunity to dial way up on your creativity. Choose two or three words, and pick a picture that summarizes your new story. For some people the picture comes first, and the words follow. Either way it's totally up to you.

These aren't just words that sound good or that you saw on a poster with someone in the background climbing a mountain. These are words that sum up all your dreams for what your new story is going to bring to you. It's important that you take the time to think carefully about these words. Roll them around in your mind until you pick the perfect words that, when said together, get you excited, thinking about your new story.

Word	→	**Picture**
Confidence	→	You, dressed as your favorite super hero
Joyful	→	Children laughing
Peaceful	→	Watching the sunset on a beach

A few questions to get you started...

- When you think of this new story of your life that you are writing, what feelings do you have?
- When you think of who you will be in this new life, pick one word to describe who that version of you is?
- When others meet you, what key words would you like them to use to describe you?
- When you think of this new story, what picture comes to mind?
- When you see yourself fully living this new story, what does that scene look like?

"Make your vision so clear that your fears become irrelevant."
–Unknown

Summary of My New Story in...

words

1
2
3

& a picture

Feel free to draw it (stick figures welcome) or print out a picture and tape it below.

Making it Stick

Something to think about...

You made it! You're one single, tiny step away from no longer just *thinking* about your new story but actually *doing things* to make it a reality. Before we get to this final part, take some time for a dance break to celebrate the work you've already done! (I'll wait ...)

Not only are you clearer about your story and what gets in your way, you have also wrestled the pen away from those real or imaginary situations that you felt were controlling your story. You now have taken the pen firmly in hand to write the story for yourself! Understanding this and doing something about it is a HUGE step.

This final piece just helps put some additional supports in place to help cheer you on as you practice living in your new story:

- **Keep it Visible** - Where will you keep your summary words/pictures so they can help keep your new story real for you?
- **A Helping Hand** - Who can help both by encouraging you and keeping you committed to your new habits?
- **Time to Party** - How will you celebrate when you've successfully practiced your new habit?
- **A Reminder That This Isn't Forever** - When is the next date you should give your story a re-look and start on the next revision?

A few questions to get you started...

- Where is a good place that you look every day that would be an ideal location to keep your Summary visible?
- Who in your circle of friends/family/co-workers/peers will cheer you on when you need it, and give you some tough love when you're not doing the things you committed to?
- What is something you can do for yourself as a pat on the back for the hard work you're doing creating new habits? When is a good time to celebrate the new habit?
- Every story needs revisions based on how quickly you can tell if your new habits are working or not. How soon do you think you should start on your next revision?

Making it Stick
Last Piece of the Puzzle...

Keep it Visible
Where will you keep your summary words/pictures so they can help keep your new story alive for you?

Time to Party
How will you celebrate when you have successfully practiced your new habit?

A Helping Hand
Who can help both by encouraging you and keeping you committed to your new habits?

A Reminder that this isn't Forever
When is the next date you should give your story a re-look and start on the next revision? Stop RIGHT NOW and put a reminder on your calendar & the next page.

"One day? Or day one. You decide."
—Unknown

CONGRATULATIONS

to **YOU** for picking up the pen, now go write an amazing story...

Next Revision Date: _____

Let's Get to Editing

Every story (no matter how epic you thought it was when you wrote it) needs to be revised from time to time. So here is your chance to think through the last revision of your story and figure out what works for you, and what you would change.

Here is where I knocked it out of the park with my new story:

Here is what I thought would work in the new story, but it didn't:

Here is what I said I would do in the new story, but never actually followed through:

My Current Story

Something to think about...

Imagine that you are the star of your own TV series. Before jumping into planning the wardrobe and shooting locations, think of how you would introduce yourself to the audience. What description about your personality, what matters most to you, your finances, family, or work life are important for the viewers to understand as they get to know you?

I want you to take these ideas and summarize them in the box marked "My Story." You can use bulleted phrases, or individual words; it's up to you. The most important idea is that it should represent where/what you are NOW – not what you want, what you imagine, or what you think your story should be.

Next, life is complicated. And so is your story. While it may be tempting to paint your story with a broad brush as either "great" or "horrible," this is hardly ever the case. You are likely basing these large strokes on either your general personality style or the week you just had vs. reality. Truly, your story has parts that you love, and other parts you wish would just disappear.

In the other two spaces provided, I want you to push yourself to put away that broad brush and look closely at the details to discover the "Favorite Parts" and the "Sticky Situations" of your story.

A few questions to get you started...
- When you think of your story, how large a role does career, money, relationships and family play in your story?
- What makes you most proud about where you are right now?
- The last time you truly enjoyed yourself, who were you with? What did you get out of it that you would love more of?
- What *doesn't* work for you about your story?
- What was the last situation that made you cry?

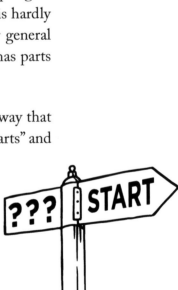

My Current Story

"Please think about your legacy because you're writing it every day."
–Gary Waynerchuck

My Story

Think where you currently are with things that are important to you (relationships, work, money, other). In phrases or single words, write your current story.

My FAVORITE Part

What makes you happy, proud or content about your story?

The STICKY Situation

What makes you sad, exhausted, or frustrated about your story?

Accomplishments

Something to think about...

Think about the next twelve months and think of four things that, once done, will make you "Ridiculously Proud". Consider this me highlighting and underlining the "Ridiculously Proud" part because it is important. These aren't goals you think you "should" have, what someone else thought would be a good idea for you, or someone else's expectations. This is something that deep down will make you jump for joy at putting them on the "Done" list.

So, with this excitement factor in mind, let's take a minute to talk about how to help you express this accomplishment. A common acronym used related to goals is SMART (*Specific, Measurable, Actionable, Realistic, Time Bound*). In this part, we will focus on Specific, Measurable, and Timebound when writing these accomplishments that will make you "Ridiculously Proud."

Start with **Specific** – clear/short (*example:* "I will be more financially responsible")

Add in **Measurable** – clearly know if you did it or not (*example:* "I will be more financially responsible by saving $500 to a separate emergency fund account.")

Tie it off with **Time Specific** – when you will be done (*example:* "I will be more financially responsible by saving $500 to a separate emergency fund by December 31st, 2019.")

Now you are ready to get going. Once you complete the list, look back over it. And if you aren't excited, you still have some thinking to do.

A few questions to get you started...

- What is your proudest accomplishment in life so far? What made it so memorable?
- What dream have you put off for too long?
- On a scale of one to ten, how would you rate your career, money, health, relationships? What accomplishment would make any of them a *fifteen*?
- What accomplishment have you thought, "There is no way I have the time or money to do that"?
- If someone were to write a news article about you in a year, what would you want it to say?

  # Accomplishments

Specific	Measurable	Time Specific
Clear/Short	Clearly know if you did it or not	When will you be done

On a scale of 1-10, how excited are you about this list? ☐

"What accomplishment(s) would make you RIDICULOUSLY PROUD?"
-Karen Eber

Clean Up Time

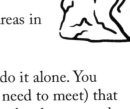

Something to think about...

Time to face up to those "Sticky Parts" of your story. No longer going the easy way of dodging them because either you don't have the energy to deal with them, or you are hoping they'll somehow magically disappear on their own. As you face them, also want you to avoid the temptation of just thinking about what makes them so sticky. Instead, focus on what you can actually do about them.

When thinking through how you can start to clean up these areas in your life, think about it in a few ways:

- **People** – Often the biggest hurdle is thinking you have to do it alone. You don't. There are people out there (that you already know or need to meet) that would enthusiastically help you. You just have to figure out who they are and then speak up and ask them for help.
- **Think/Say** – You have likely been telling yourself (and others) over and over again why this situation won't change. Here, write what NEW words/thoughts you will use to replace those old ones with that aren't helping you.
- **Get Moving** – What are the two things you can immediately do *this week* to begin cleaning up these situations?

A few questions to get you started...

- What would your life be like if these situations were gone?
- Who do you already know or would like to meet that could help you with the situation?
- Who can you ask for help?
- How do any of these "Sticky Situations" get in the way of the "Ridiculously Proud" accomplishments you listed?
- What have you been telling yourself about this situation? And how is that helping or hurting you getting past these "Sticky Situations"?

"The question isn't who is going to let me; it's who is going to stop me."
-Ayn Rand

Clean Up Time

List a few sticky parts from your original story and brainstorm "Solutions" you can use to change them.

STICKY SITUATIONS

SOLUTIONS   SOLUTIONS   SOLUTIONS
People   People   People

Think/Say   Think/Say   Think/Say

Get Moving: List two things you can do THIS WEEK to start cleaning up these situations

Whose Life Is This Anyway?! Making Your Life Your Story

Next Stop, Your New Destination

Something to think about...

So now you have cozied up with your current story, looked at what you love and would love more of and gone deeper into what you want to change about it. Here you will consider the future, assuming that all of the "Sticky Situations" have been resolved and you have accomplished what you shared that would make you "Ridiculously Proud." Now, you will peek into the future to see what that new story is, with all of this in place.

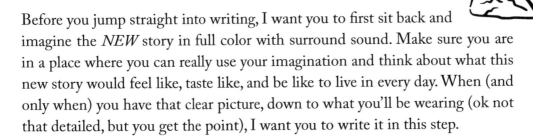

Before you jump straight into writing, I want you to first sit back and imagine the *NEW* story in full color with surround sound. Make sure you are in a place where you can really use your imagination and think about what this new story would feel like, taste like, and be like to live in every day. When (and only when) you have that clear picture, down to what you'll be wearing (ok not that detailed, but you get the point), I want you to write it in this step.

IMPORTANT: While technically you are writing this step as a future goal, you will write it in the present tense AS IF IT IS ALREADY TRUE. Use language like "I am" instead of "I will be"; and use "I have" instead of "I would have." By writing it in the present tense, it will begin to be more real to you.

A few questions to get you started...

- If you could talk to yourself 10 years in the future, what would that version of you say?
- If you weren't concerned about what anyone else thought, what would be your perfect story?
- Stepping into this new story, what feelings are there?
- Think of someone you admire. What about their story makes you want to be around them?
- With the "Ridiculously Proud" accomplishments behind you, what additional accomplishments would you now be ready for?

Next Stop, your NEW Destination

My NEW Story

Describe the future assuming that all of the "Sticky Situations" have been resolved, and you have accomplished what you shared that would make you "Ridiculously Proud".

A Day in the Life

Describe a day in the life of your new story?

I'm PROUD...

What about this NEW story makes you most proud?

"When writing the story of your life, don't let anyone else hold the pen." –Unknown

Distractions

Something to think about...

With every amazing story, there are countless things lurking around every corner to distract you. The best way to stick to your plan is to already know they are coming and find ways to remind yourself of why your new story is more important than the distractions. While you can't plan for everything, you can spend time now thinking through some of the obvious ones, so you'll be ready.

Here is a good chance to look back at any of those "Sticky Situations" to see if they are getting in the way of your new story, and what you will do about them when they show up.

Hint: They are likely to be some things that are already standing in between you and your new story by sucking up your time but not getting you anywhere closer to your goals.

Another Hint: People/situations can be distractions.

A few questions to get you started...

- Think of the last time you felt yourself fully *in the zone*. What was it about your environment that helped you focus?
- How does the way you spend your time each day line up to the priorities you have for your life?
- The last time you sat down to accomplish a goal, what stopped you or slowed you down?
- How much time do you spend each day on social media or watching TV? Are you comfortable with the answer?
- When distractions come up, how will you show that you are committed to your goals?

Distractions

"Starve your distractions feed your focus."
—Unknown

List five distractions that are likely coming your way to throw you off your story.

1

2

3

4

5

 How will you remind yourself that your story is more important than the distractions above?

Out With the Old

Something to think about...

Habits are wonderful things – until they get in the way of your story! Just like clothes, sometimes you outgrow your habits too. But instead of getting rid of them, you keep trying to stuff your life into them, even though they aren't comfortable and no longer make you look good. Now, think through your current habits and find those that no longer work for your new story. In addition to the habit, write out what it is about that habit that doesn't line up with the new story you came up with.

Hint: Thoughts can be habits too.

Current Habit	→	**How it Doesn't Line up to my New Story**
Eating out every day for lunch	→	That money could be used to build up my savings account.
Thinking that "I'm not creative"	→	Stops me from trying new things.
Too much time on my phone	→	Takes away time from the development of my new business.

A few questions to get you started...

- What habits do you have that have added to or helped create the "Sticky Situations" in your life?
- What habits have you had over the last five years that haven't changed, even though your life has changed?
- What habits have you been "meaning to," "thinking about" or "trying" to change?
- When you think about people around you, what habits have you picked up from them that don't line up with your new story?
- What current habit is the largest barrier to you moving into your new story?

Out With the Old...
Standing between me and my new story

What HABITS have to go away?

 How does this old habit get in the way of your new story?

> "If you want something new, you have to stop doing something old." –Peter Drucker

In With the New

Something to think about...

Things happen, and stories change because you actually do something different, not because you think about changing them, would like to change them, or consider changing them. Hands down, the best way to bring your new story to life is by creating habits that line up with the story. Every day you are either reinforcing an old habit or creating a new habit. Period. There is no neutral. While you are "thinking about" or "maybe starting" the new habit, you are highlighting, underlining, and becoming more comfortable in your current habit.

Go back and refresh yourself on your new story. Take the time to fully remember not only what that new story looks like on you, but what it feels like, and what a day in the life of that story would be like. Then come back and write down three or four new habits that you will do daily, weekly, or monthly which will get you to start living this story today. As you think about these habits, make sure they are measurable. Here are a few examples:

Goal (not easy to measure)	→	**Habit (easy to measure)**
Be healthier	→	Go to the gym 3 times a week
Save more money	→	Add $25 per paycheck to my savings account
Spend less time watching TV	→	Watch 2 hours (or less) of TV a day

Keep it to three or four because tackling too many new habits at once can be overwhelming and **then you give up**. Also, tackling too few habits will make it impossible to see how you are getting closer to your story, and **then you give up** (*see the theme here?*). So, stick to three or four to get some progress. Remember, in writing your story there will be many chances for revision, so don't feel like you need to change everything at once. What is important is what you can do **consistently**.

A few questions to get you started...

- What is that habit you have been "thinking about" starting for a while that lines up to your new story?
- When you think through what a day in the life of your new story would look like, what do you see yourself doing every day?
- What habits do you admire in others that line up with your story?
- With the bad habits you committed to stopping now gone, what new habits do you have space for?
- What is the one habit that would make you most proud of your progress?

In With the NEW...

Write a few habits that you will start doing daily/weekly/monthly/etc. to make your new story real:

Goal	New Habit	How Often?

"Successful people are simply those with successful habits." –Brian Tracy

Keeping an Eye on Your Habits

Something to think about...

Now that you have zeroed in on the new habits that will help bring your story to life, let's talk about how you will see if you are actually practicing them. Unfortunately, just asking yourself won't work because memory (*not just yours, but everyone's*) is unreliable. All people (*you included*) tend to flavor the answer with what they *would like to believe* about themselves. This either leads to giving more credit than is deserved or being a harsher judge than necessary. Here we just want to be accurate, for better or worse, so we can understand if the change is actually working (*Yeah!*) or if a revision is needed (*Aw! But that's ok too*).

Since we can't rely on your faulty memory, in this step you will think through (*and set up*) ways that you plan to track those new habits. This is your chance to be creative. You don't only want to track them, but you want to track them in a way that gets you excited to do it and stay consistent.

Some inspiration to get you started...

- Do a web search for "Habit Trackers," and you will get an abundance of ideas, everything from the simple to the beautifully artistic. Find a few that get you excited.

- Write a simple checklist of your new habits and keep it clearly visible (*think refrigerator, bathroom sink, above your desk, screen saver on your phone*) of your new habits. Physically check them off as you practice the habit.

- Re-live grade school and creatively decorate one index card for each habit. Then hang them somewhere you will see them often throughout the day.

- Get a journal specifically for writing down a few lines at the end of every day, and grade yourself on how you are doing against your new habits.

- Find someone to partner with on the goal/habit so you both can help keep each other on track.

Keeping an Eye on Your Habits

"A goal without a plan is just a wish."
—Antoine de Saint-Exupéry

Get creative on how you will keep your new habits front and center, and how you can tell if you actually are doing them.

New Habit	How will you keep track if you did it or not?	Have you created the tracker?
		☐ yes
		☐ yes
		☐ yes
		☐ yes

In Summary

Something to think about...

Now comes the time to begin to wrap up your new story with a lovely big bow. It's time to summarize your new story in such a neon-colored way that when you're tempted to slip back into old habits or need convincing why the effort will be worth it in the end, you have something short and sweet to help snap you back. Think of this as the shorthand representation of your new story.

Here's another opportunity to dial way up on your creativity. Choose two or three words, and pick a picture that summarizes your new story. For some people the picture comes first, and the words follow. Either way it's totally up to you.

These aren't just words that sound good or that you saw on a poster with someone in the background climbing a mountain. These are words that sum up all your dreams for what your new story is going to bring to you. It's important that you take the time to think carefully about these words. Roll them around in your mind until you pick the perfect words that, when said together, get you excited, thinking about your new story.

Word	→	**Picture**
Confidence	→	You, dressed as your favorite super hero
Joyful	→	Children laughing
Peaceful	→	Watching the sunset on a beach

A few questions to get you started...

- When you think of this new story of your life that you are writing, what feelings do you have?
- When you think of who you will be in this new life, pick one word to describe who that version of you is?
- When others meet you, what key words would you like them to use to describe you?
- When you think of this new story, what picture comes to mind?
- When you see yourself fully living this new story, what does that scene look like?

Summary of My New Story in...

words

1
2
3

& a picture

Feel free to draw it (stick figures welcome) or print out a picture and tape it below.

"Make your vision so clear that your fears become irrelevant."
—Unknown

Making it Stick

Something to think about...

You made it! You're one single, tiny step away from no longer just *thinking* about your new story but actually *doing things* to make it a reality. Before we get to this final part, take some time for a dance break to celebrate the work you've already done! (I'll wait . . .)

Not only are you clearer about your story and what gets in your way, you have also wrestled the pen away from those real or imaginary situations that you felt were controlling your story. You now have taken the pen firmly in hand to write the story for yourself! Understanding this and doing something about it is a HUGE step.

This final piece just helps put some additional supports in place to help cheer you on as you practice living in your new story:

- **Keep it Visible** - Where will you keep your summary words/pictures so they can help keep your new story real for you?
- **A Helping Hand** - Who can help both by encouraging you and keeping you committed to your new habits?
- **Time to Party** - How will you celebrate when you've successfully practiced your new habit?
- **A Reminder That This Isn't Forever** - When is the next date you should give your story a re-look and start on the next revision?

A few questions to get you started...

- Where is a good place that you look every day that would be an ideal location to keep your Summary visible?
- Who in your circle of friends/family/co-workers/peers will cheer you on when you need it, and give you some tough love when you're not doing the things you committed to?
- What is something you can do for yourself as a pat on the back for the hard work you're doing creating new habits? When is a good time to celebrate the new habit?
- Every story needs revisions based on how quickly you can tell if your new habits are working or not. How soon do you think you should start on your next revision?

Making it Stick
Last Piece of the Puzzle...

Keep it Visible
Where will you keep your summary words/pictures so they can help keep your new story alive for you?

Time to Party
How will you celebrate when you have successfully practiced your new habit?

A Helping Hand
Who can help both by encouraging you and keeping you committed to your new habits?

A Reminder that this isn't Forever
When is the next date you should give your story a re-look and start on the next revision? Stop RIGHT NOW and put a reminder on your calendar & the next page.

"One day? Or day one. You decide."
—Unknown

CONGRATULATIONS

to YOU for picking up the pen, now go write an amazing story...

Next Revision Date: _____

Let's Get to Editing

Every story (no matter how epic you thought it was when you wrote it) needs to be revised from time to time. So here is your chance to think through the last revision of your story and figure out what works for you, and what you would change.

Here is where I knocked it out of the park with my new story:

Here is what I thought would work in the new story, but it didn't:

Here is what I said I would do in the new story, but never actually followed through:

My Current Story

Something to think about...

Imagine that you are the star of your own TV series. Before jumping into planning the wardrobe and shooting locations, think of how you would introduce yourself to the audience. What description about your personality, what matters most to you, your finances, family, or work life are important for the viewers to understand as they get to know you?

I want you to take these ideas and summarize them in the box marked "My Story." You can use bulleted phrases, or individual words; it's up to you. The most important idea is that it should represent where/what you are NOW – not what you want, what you imagine, or what you think your story should be.

Next, life is complicated. And so is your story. While it may be tempting to paint your story with a broad brush as either "great" or "horrible," this is hardly ever the case. You are likely basing these large strokes on either your general personality style or the week you just had vs. reality. Truly, your story has parts that you love, and other parts you wish would just disappear.

In the other two spaces provided, I want you to push yourself to put away that broad brush and look closely at the details to discover the "Favorite Parts" and the "Sticky Situations" of your story.

A few questions to get you started...
- When you think of your story, how large a role does career, money, relationships and family play in your story?
- What makes you most proud about where you are right now?
- The last time you truly enjoyed yourself, who were you with? What did you get out of it that you would love more of?
- What *doesn't* work for you about your story?
- What was the last situation that made you cry?

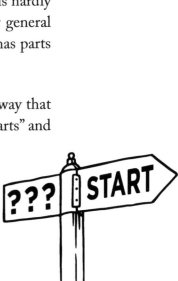

My Current Story

"Please think about your legacy because you're writing it every day."
—Gary Waynerchuck

My Story

Think where you currently are with things that are important to you (relationships, work, money, other). In phrases or single words, write your current story.

My FAVORITE Part

What makes you happy, proud or content about your story?

The STICKY Situation

What makes you sad, exhausted, or frustrated about your story?

Accomplishments

Something to think about...

Think about the next twelve months and think of four things that, once done, will make you "Ridiculously Proud". Consider this me highlighting and underlining the "Ridiculously Proud" part because it is important. These aren't goals you think you "should" have, what someone else thought would be a good idea for you, or someone else's expectations. This is something that deep down will make you jump for joy at putting them on the "Done" list.

So, with this excitement factor in mind, let's take a minute to talk about how to help you express this accomplishment. A common acronym used related to goals is SMART (*Specific, Measurable, Actionable, Realistic, Time Bound*). In this part, we will focus on Specific, Measurable, and Timebound when writing these accomplishments that will make you "Ridiculously Proud."

Start with **Specific** – clear/short (*example:* "I will be more financially responsible")

Add in **Measurable** – clearly know if you did it or not (*example:* "I will be more financially responsible by saving $500 to a separate emergency fund account.")

Tie it off with **Time Specific** – when you will be done (*example:* "I will be more financially responsible by saving $500 to a separate emergency fund by December 31st, 2019.")

Now you are ready to get going. Once you complete the list, look back over it. And if you aren't excited, you still have some thinking to do.

A few questions to get you started...
- What is your proudest accomplishment in life so far? What made it so memorable?
- What dream have you put off for too long?
- On a scale of one to ten, how would you rate your career, money, health, relationships? What accomplishment would make any of them a *fifteen*?
- What accomplishment have you thought, "There is no way I have the time or money to do that"?
- If someone were to write a news article about you in a year, what would you want it to say?

Accomplishments

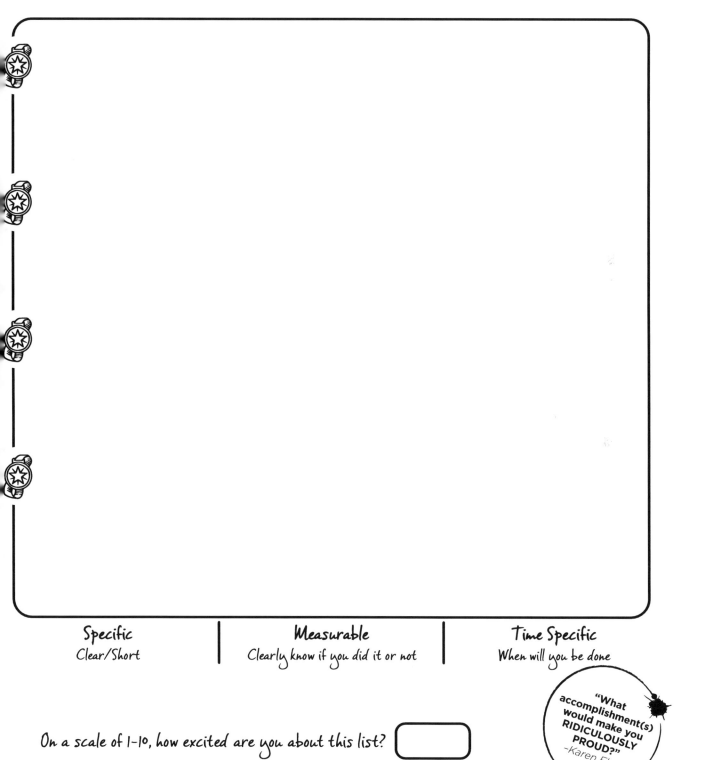

Specific	Measurable	Time Specific
Clear/Short	Clearly know if you did it or not	When will you be done

On a scale of 1-10, how excited are you about this list? ☐

"What accomplishment(s) would make you RIDICULOUSLY PROUD?"
–Karen Eber

Clean Up Time

Something to think about...

Time to face up to those "Sticky Parts" of your story. No longer going the easy way of dodging them because either you don't have the energy to deal with them, or you are hoping they'll somehow magically disappear on their own. As you face them, also want you to avoid the temptation of just thinking about what makes them so sticky. Instead, focus on what you can actually do about them.

When thinking through how you can start to clean up these areas in your life, think about it in a few ways:

- **People** – Often the biggest hurdle is thinking you have to do it alone. You don't. There are people out there (that you already know or need to meet) that would enthusiastically help you. You just have to figure out who they are and then speak up and ask them for help.
- **Think/Say** – You have likely been telling yourself (and others) over and over again why this situation won't change. Here, write what NEW words/thoughts you will use to replace those old ones with that aren't helping you.
- **Get Moving** – What are the two things you can immediately do *this week* to begin cleaning up these situations?

A few questions to get you started...

- What would your life be like if these situations were gone?
- Who do you already know or would like to meet that could help you with the situation?
- Who can you ask for help?
- How do any of these "Sticky Situations" get in the way of the "Ridiculously Proud" accomplishments you listed?
- What have you been telling yourself about this situation? And how is that helping or hurting you getting past these "Sticky Situations"?

"The question isn't who is going to let me; it's who is going to stop me."
—Ayn Rand

Clean Up Time

List a few sticky parts from your original story and brainstorm "Solutions" you can use to change them.

STICKY SITUATIONS

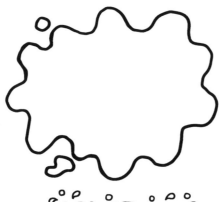
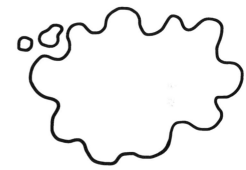

SOLUTIONS   SOLUTIONS   SOLUTIONS

People   People   People

Think/Say   Think/Say   Think/Say

Get Moving: List two things you can do THIS WEEK to start cleaning up these situations

Next Stop, Your New Destination

Something to think about...

So now you have cozied up with your current story, looked at what you love and would love more of and gone deeper into what you want to change about it. Here you will consider the future, assuming that all of the "Sticky Situations" have been resolved and you have accomplished what you shared that would make you "Ridiculously Proud." Now, you will peek into the future to see what that new story is, with all of this in place.

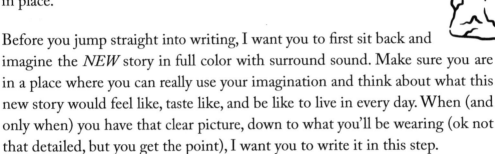

Before you jump straight into writing, I want you to first sit back and imagine the *NEW* story in full color with surround sound. Make sure you are in a place where you can really use your imagination and think about what this new story would feel like, taste like, and be like to live in every day. When (and only when) you have that clear picture, down to what you'll be wearing (ok not that detailed, but you get the point), I want you to write it in this step.

IMPORTANT: While technically you are writing this step as a future goal, you will write it in the present tense AS IF IT IS ALREADY TRUE. Use language like "I am" instead of "I will be"; and use "I have" instead of "I would have." By writing it in the present tense, it will begin to be more real to you.

A few questions to get you started...

- If you could talk to yourself 10 years in the future, what would that version of you say?
- If you weren't concerned about what anyone else thought, what would be your perfect story?
- Stepping into this new story, what feelings are there?
- Think of someone you admire. What about their story makes you want to be around them?
- With the "Ridiculously Proud" accomplishments behind you, what additional accomplishments would you now be ready for?

Next Stop, your NEW Destination

My NEW Story

Describe the future assuming that all of the "Sticky Situations" have been resolved, and you have accomplished what you shared that would make you "Ridiculously Proud".

A Day in the Life

Describe a day in the life of your new story?

I'm PROUD...

What about this NEW story makes you most proud?

> "When writing the story of your life, don't let anyone else hold the pen." —Unknown

Distractions

Something to think about...

With every amazing story, there are countless things lurking around every corner to distract you. The best way to stick to your plan is to already know they are coming and find ways to remind yourself of why your new story is more important than the distractions. While you can't plan for everything, you can spend time now thinking through some of the obvious ones, so you'll be ready.

Here is a good chance to look back at any of those "Sticky Situations" to see if they are getting in the way of your new story, and what you will do about them when they show up.

Hint: They are likely to be some things that are already standing in between you and your new story by sucking up your time but not getting you anywhere closer to your goals.

Another Hint: People/situations can be distractions.

A few questions to get you started...

- Think of the last time you felt yourself fully *in the zone*. What was it about your environment that helped you focus?
- How does the way you spend your time each day line up to the priorities you have for your life?
- The last time you sat down to accomplish a goal, what stopped you or slowed you down?
- How much time do you spend each day on social media or watching TV? Are you comfortable with the answer?
- When distractions come up, how will you show that you are committed to your goals?

Distractions

"Starve your distractions feed your focus." —Unknown

List five distractions that are likely coming your way to throw you off your story.

1
2
3
4
5

How will you remind yourself that your story is more important than the distractions above?

Out With the Old

Something to think about...

Habits are wonderful things – until they get in the way of your story! Just like clothes, sometimes you outgrow your habits too. But instead of getting rid of them, you keep trying to stuff your life into them, even though they aren't comfortable and no longer make you look good. Now, think through your current habits and find those that no longer work for your new story. In addition to the habit, write out what it is about that habit that doesn't line up with the new story you came up with.

Hint: Thoughts can be habits too.

Current Habit	→	**How it Doesn't Line up to my New Story**
Eating out every day for lunch	→	That money could be used to build up my savings account.
Thinking that "I'm not creative"	→	Stops me from trying new things.
Too much time on my phone	→	Takes away time from the development of my new business.

A few questions to get you started...

- What habits do you have that have added to or helped create the "Sticky Situations" in your life?
- What habits have you had over the last five years that haven't changed, even though your life has changed?
- What habits have you been "meaning to," "thinking about" or "trying" to change?
- When you think about people around you, what habits have you picked up from them that don't line up with your new story?
- What current habit is the largest barrier to you moving into your new story?

Out With the Old...
Standing between me and my new story

What HABITS have to go away?

 How does this old habit get in the way of your new story?

> "If you want something new, you have to stop doing something old." –Peter Drucker

In With the New

Something to think about...

Things happen, and stories change because you actually do something different, not because you think about changing them, would like to change them, or consider changing them. Hands down, the best way to bring your new story to life is by creating habits that line up with the story. Every day you are either reinforcing an old habit or creating a new habit. Period. There is no neutral. While you are "thinking about" or "maybe starting" the new habit, you are highlighting, underlining, and becoming more comfortable in your current habit.

Go back and refresh yourself on your new story. Take the time to fully remember not only what that new story looks like on you, but what it feels like, and what a day in the life of that story would be like. Then come back and write down three or four new habits that you will do daily, weekly, or monthly which will get you to start living this story today. As you think about these habits, make sure they are measurable. Here are a few examples:

Goal (not easy to measure) →	**Habit (easy to measure)**
Be healthier →	Go to the gym 3 times a week
Save more money →	Add $25 per paycheck to my savings account
Spend less time watching TV →	Watch 2 hours (or less) of TV a day

Keep it to three or four because tackling too many new habits at once can be overwhelming and **then you give up**. Also, tackling too few habits will make it impossible to see how you are getting closer to your story, and **then you give up** (*see the theme here?*). So, stick to three or four to get some progress. Remember, in writing your story there will be many chances for revision, so don't feel like you need to change everything at once. What is important is what you can do **consistently**.

A few questions to get you started...

- What is that habit you have been "thinking about" starting for a while that lines up to your new story?
- When you think through what a day in the life of your new story would look like, what do you see yourself doing every day?
- What habits do you admire in others that line up with your story?
- With the bad habits you committed to stopping now gone, what new habits do you have space for?
- What is the one habit that would make you most proud of your progress?

In With the NEW...

Write a few habits that you will start doing daily/weekly/monthly/etc. to make your new story real:

Goal	New Habit	How Often?

"Successful people are simply those with successful habits." –Brian Tracy

Keeping an Eye on Your Habits

Something to think about...

Now that you have zeroed in on the new habits that will help bring your story to life, let's talk about how you will see if you are actually practicing them. Unfortunately, just asking yourself won't work because memory (*not just yours, but everyone's*) is unreliable. All people (*you included*) tend to flavor the answer with what they *would like to believe* about themselves. This either leads to giving more credit than is deserved or being a harsher judge than necessary. Here we just want to be accurate, for better or worse, so we can understand if the change is actually working (*Yeah!*) or if a revision is needed (*Aw! But that's ok too*).

Since we can't rely on your faulty memory, in this step you will think through (*and set up*) ways that you plan to track those new habits. This is your chance to be creative. You don't only want to track them, but you want to track them in a way that gets you excited to do it and stay consistent.

Some inspiration to get you started...

- Do a web search for "Habit Trackers," and you will get an abundance of ideas, everything from the simple to the beautifully artistic. Find a few that get you excited.
- Write a simple checklist of your new habits and keep it clearly visible (*think refrigerator, bathroom sink, above your desk, screen saver on your phone*) of your new habits. Physically check them off as you practice the habit.
- Re-live grade school and creatively decorate one index card for each habit. Then hang them somewhere you will see them often throughout the day.
- Get a journal specifically for writing down a few lines at the end of every day, and grade yourself on how you are doing against your new habits.
- Find someone to partner with on the goal/habit so you both can help keep each other on track.

Keeping an Eye on Your Habits

"A goal without a plan is just a wish."
—Antoine de Saint-Exupéry

Get creative on how you will keep your new habits front and center, and how you can tell if you actually are doing them.

New Habit	How will you keep track if you did it or not?	Have you created the tracker?
		☐ yes
		☐ yes
		☐ yes
		☐ yes

Whose Life Is This Anyway?! Making Your Life Your Story

In Summary

Something to think about...

Now comes the time to begin to wrap up your new story with a lovely big bow. It's time to summarize your new story in such a neon-colored way that when you're tempted to slip back into old habits or need convincing why the effort will be worth it in the end, you have something short and sweet to help snap you back. Think of this as the shorthand representation of your new story.

Here's another opportunity to dial way up on your creativity. Choose two or three words, and pick a picture that summarizes your new story. For some people the picture comes first, and the words follow. Either way it's totally up to you.

These aren't just words that sound good or that you saw on a poster with someone in the background climbing a mountain. These are words that sum up all your dreams for what your new story is going to bring to you. It's important that you take the time to think carefully about these words. Roll them around in your mind until you pick the perfect words that, when said together, get you excited, thinking about your new story.

Word	→	**Picture**
Confidence	→	You, dressed as your favorite super hero
Joyful	→	Children laughing
Peaceful	→	Watching the sunset on a beach

A few questions to get you started...

- When you think of this new story of your life that you are writing, what feelings do you have?
- When you think of who you will be in this new life, pick one word to describe who that version of you is?
- When others meet you, what key words would you like them to use to describe you?
- When you think of this new story, what picture comes to mind?
- When you see yourself fully living this new story, what does that scene look like?

Summary of My New Story in...

words

1
2
3

& a picture

Feel free to draw it (stick figures welcome) or print out a picture and tape it below.

"Make your vision so clear that your fears become irrelevant."
–Unknown

Making it Stick

Something to think about...

You made it! You're one single, tiny step away from no longer just *thinking* about your new story but actually *doing things* to make it a reality. Before we get to this final part, take some time for a dance break to celebrate the work you've already done! (I'll wait . . .)

Not only are you clearer about your story and what gets in your way, you have also wrestled the pen away from those real or imaginary situations that you felt were controlling your story. You now have taken the pen firmly in hand to write the story for yourself! Understanding this and doing something about it is a HUGE step.

This final piece just helps put some additional supports in place to help cheer you on as you practice living in your new story:

- **Keep it Visible** - Where will you keep your summary words/pictures so they can help keep your new story real for you?
- **A Helping Hand** - Who can help both by encouraging you and keeping you committed to your new habits?
- **Time to Party** - How will you celebrate when you've successfully practiced your new habit?
- **A Reminder That This Isn't Forever** - When is the next date you should give your story a re-look and start on the next revision?

A few questions to get you started...

- Where is a good place that you look every day that would be an ideal location to keep your Summary visible?
- Who in your circle of friends/family/co-workers/peers will cheer you on when you need it, and give you some tough love when you're not doing the things you committed to?
- What is something you can do for yourself as a pat on the back for the hard work you're doing creating new habits? When is a good time to celebrate the new habit?
- Every story needs revisions based on how quickly you can tell if your new habits are working or not. How soon do you think you should start on your next revision?

Making it Stick
Last Piece of the Puzzle...

Keep it Visible
Where will you keep your summary words/pictures so they can help keep your new story alive for you?

Time to Party
How will you celebrate when you have successfully practiced your new habit?

A Helping Hand
Who can help both by encouraging you and keeping you committed to your new habits?

A Reminder that this isn't Forever
When is the next date you should give your story a re-look and start on the next revision? Stop RIGHT NOW and put a reminder on your calendar & the next page.

"One day? Or day one. You decide."
—Unknown

CONGRATULATIONS

to YOU for picking up the pen, now go write an amazing story...

Next Revision Date: _____

Let's Get to Editing

Every story (no matter how epic you thought it was when you wrote it) needs to be revised from time to time. So here is your chance to think through the last revision of your story and figure out what works for you, and what you would change.

Here is where I knocked it out of the park with my new story:

Here is what I thought would work in the new story, but it didn't:

Here is what I said I would do in the new story, but never actually followed through:

My Current Story

Something to think about...

Imagine that you are the star of your own TV series. Before jumping into planning the wardrobe and shooting locations, think of how you would introduce yourself to the audience. What description about your personality, what matters most to you, your finances, family, or work life are important for the viewers to understand as they get to know you?

I want you to take these ideas and summarize them in the box marked "My Story." You can use bulleted phrases, or individual words; it's up to you. The most important idea is that it should represent where/what you are NOW – not what you want, what you imagine, or what you think your story should be.

Next, life is complicated. And so is your story. While it may be tempting to paint your story with a broad brush as either "great" or "horrible," this is hardly ever the case. You are likely basing these large strokes on either your general personality style or the week you just had vs. reality. Truly, your story has parts that you love, and other parts you wish would just disappear.

In the other two spaces provided, I want you to push yourself to put away that broad brush and look closely at the details to discover the "Favorite Parts" and the "Sticky Situations" of your story.

A few questions to get you started...

- When you think of your story, how large a role does career, money, relationships and family play in your story?
- What makes you most proud about where you are right now?
- The last time you truly enjoyed yourself, who were you with? What did you get out of it that you would love more of?
- What *doesn't* work for you about your story?
- What was the last situation that made you cry?

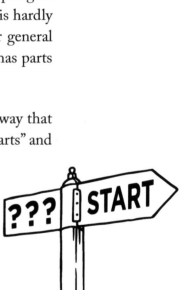

My Current Story

"Please think about your legacy because you're writing it every day."
–Gary Waynerchuck

My Story

Think where you currently are with things that are important to you (relationships, work, money, other). In phrases or single words, write your current story.

My FAVORITE Part

What makes you happy, proud or content about your story?

The STICKY Situation

What makes you sad, exhausted, or frustrated about your story?

Accomplishments

Something to think about...

Think about the next twelve months and think of four things that, once done, will make you "Ridiculously Proud". Consider this me highlighting and underlining the "Ridiculously Proud" part because it is important. These aren't goals you think you "should" have, what someone else thought would be a good idea for you, or someone else's expectations. This is something that deep down will make you jump for joy at putting them on the "Done" list.

So, with this excitement factor in mind, let's take a minute to talk about how to help you express this accomplishment. A common acronym used related to goals is SMART (*Specific, Measurable, Actionable, Realistic, Time Bound*). In this part, we will focus on Specific, Measurable, and Timebound when writing these accomplishments that will make you "Ridiculously Proud."

Start with **Specific** – clear/short (*example:* "I will be more financially responsible")

Add in **Measurable** – clearly know if you did it or not (*example:* "I will be more financially responsible by saving $500 to a separate emergency fund account.")

Tie it off with **Time Specific** – when you will be done (*example:* "I will be more financially responsible by saving $500 to a separate emergency fund by December 31st, 2019.")

Now you are ready to get going. Once you complete the list, look back over it. And if you aren't excited, you still have some thinking to do.

A few questions to get you started...

- What is your proudest accomplishment in life so far? What made it so memorable?
- What dream have you put off for too long?
- On a scale of one to ten, how would you rate your career, money, health, relationships? What accomplishment would make any of them a *fifteen*?
- What accomplishment have you thought, "There is no way I have the time or money to do that"?
- If someone were to write a news article about you in a year, what would you want it to say?

Accomplishments

Specific	Measurable	Time Specific
Clear/Short	Clearly know if you did it or not	When will you be done

On a scale of 1-10, how excited are you about this list? ☐

"What accomplishment(s) would make you RIDICULOUSLY PROUD?"
–Karen Eber

Clean Up Time

Something to think about...

Time to face up to those "Sticky Parts" of your story. No longer going the easy way of dodging them because either you don't have the energy to deal with them, or you are hoping they'll somehow magically disappear on their own. As you face them, also want you to avoid the temptation of just thinking about what makes them so sticky. Instead, focus on what you can actually do about them.

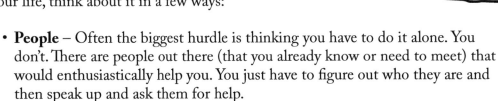

When thinking through how you can start to clean up these areas in your life, think about it in a few ways:

- **People** – Often the biggest hurdle is thinking you have to do it alone. You don't. There are people out there (that you already know or need to meet) that would enthusiastically help you. You just have to figure out who they are and then speak up and ask them for help.
- **Think/Say** – You have likely been telling yourself (and others) over and over again why this situation won't change. Here, write what NEW words/thoughts you will use to replace those old ones with that aren't helping you.
- **Get Moving** – What are the two things you can immediately do *this week* to begin cleaning up these situations?

A few questions to get you started...

- What would your life be like if these situations were gone?
- Who do you already know or would like to meet that could help you with the situation?
- Who can you ask for help?
- How do any of these "Sticky Situations" get in the way of the "Ridiculously Proud" accomplishments you listed?
- What have you been telling yourself about this situation? And how is that helping or hurting you getting past these "Sticky Situations"?

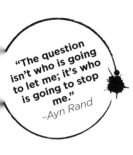
"The question isn't who is going to let me; it's who is going to stop me."
—Ayn Rand

Clean Up Time

List a few sticky parts from your original story and brainstorm "Solutions" you can use to change them.

STICKY SITUATIONS

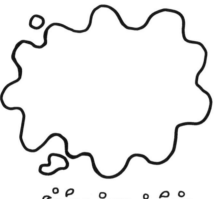
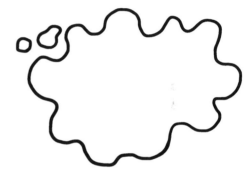

SOLUTIONS   SOLUTIONS   SOLUTIONS

People   People   People

Think/Say   Think/Say   Think/Say

Get Moving: List two things you can do THIS WEEK to start cleaning up these situations

Next Stop, Your New Destination

Something to think about...

So now you have cozied up with your current story, looked at what you love and would love more of and gone deeper into what you want to change about it. Here you will consider the future, assuming that all of the "Sticky Situations" have been resolved and you have accomplished what you shared that would make you "Ridiculously Proud." Now, you will peek into the future to see what that new story is, with all of this in place.

Before you jump straight into writing, I want you to first sit back and imagine the *NEW* story in full color with surround sound. Make sure you are in a place where you can really use your imagination and think about what this new story would feel like, taste like, and be like to live in every day. When (and only when) you have that clear picture, down to what you'll be wearing (ok not that detailed, but you get the point), I want you to write it in this step.

IMPORTANT: While technically you are writing this step as a future goal, you will write it in the present tense AS IF IT IS ALREADY TRUE. Use language like "I am" instead of "I will be"; and use "I have" instead of "I would have." By writing it in the present tense, it will begin to be more real to you.

A few questions to get you started...

- If you could talk to yourself 10 years in the future, what would that version of you say?
- If you weren't concerned about what anyone else thought, what would be your perfect story?
- Stepping into this new story, what feelings are there?
- Think of someone you admire. What about their story makes you want to be around them?
- With the "Ridiculously Proud" accomplishments behind you, what additional accomplishments would you now be ready for?

Next Stop, your NEW Destination

My NEW Story

Describe the future assuming that all of the "Sticky Situations" have been resolved, and you have accomplished what you shared that would make you "Ridiculously Proud".

A Day in the Life

Describe a day in the life of your new story?

I'm PROUD...

What about this NEW story makes you most proud?

"When writing the story of your life, don't let anyone else hold the pen." —Unknown

Distractions

Something to think about...

With every amazing story, there are countless things lurking around every corner to distract you. The best way to stick to your plan is to already know they are coming and find ways to remind yourself of why your new story is more important than the distractions. While you can't plan for everything, you can spend time now thinking through some of the obvious ones, so you'll be ready.

Here is a good chance to look back at any of those "Sticky Situations" to see if they are getting in the way of your new story, and what you will do about them when they show up.

Hint: They are likely to be some things that are already standing in between you and your new story by sucking up your time but not getting you anywhere closer to your goals.

Another Hint: People/situations can be distractions.

A few questions to get you started...

- Think of the last time you felt yourself fully *in the zone*. What was it about your environment that helped you focus?
- How does the way you spend your time each day line up to the priorities you have for your life?
- The last time you sat down to accomplish a goal, what stopped you or slowed you down?
- How much time do you spend each day on social media or watching TV? Are you comfortable with the answer?
- When distractions come up, how will you show that you are committed to your goals?

Distractions

"Starve your distractions feed your focus." —Unknown

List five distractions that are likely coming your way to throw you off your story.

1
2
3
4
5

How will you remind yourself that your story is more important than the distractions above?

Out With the Old

Something to think about...

Habits are wonderful things – until they get in the way of your story! Just like clothes, sometimes you outgrow your habits too. But instead of getting rid of them, you keep trying to stuff your life into them, even though they aren't comfortable and no longer make you look good. Now, think through your current habits and find those that no longer work for your new story. In addition to the habit, write out what it is about that habit that doesn't line up with the new story you came up with.

Hint: Thoughts can be habits too.

Current Habit	→	**How it Doesn't Line up to my New Story**
Eating out every day for lunch	→	That money could be used to build up my savings account.
Thinking that "I'm not creative"	→	Stops me from trying new things.
Too much time on my phone	→	Takes away time from the development of my new business.

A few questions to get you started...

- What habits do you have that have added to or helped create the "Sticky Situations" in your life?
- What habits have you had over the last five years that haven't changed, even though your life has changed?
- What habits have you been "meaning to," "thinking about" or "trying" to change?
- When you think about people around you, what habits have you picked up from them that don't line up with your new story?
- What current habit is the largest barrier to you moving into your new story?

Out With the Old...
Standing between me and my new story

What HABITS have to go away?

 How does this old habit get in the way of your new story?

> "If you want something new, you have to stop doing something old." –Peter Drucker

In With the New

Something to think about...

Things happen, and stories change because you actually do something different, not because you think about changing them, would like to change them, or consider changing them. Hands down, the best way to bring your new story to life is by creating habits that line up with the story. Every day you are either reinforcing an old habit or creating a new habit. Period. There is no neutral. While you are "thinking about" or "maybe starting" the new habit, you are highlighting, underlining, and becoming more comfortable in your current habit.

Go back and refresh yourself on your new story. Take the time to fully remember not only what that new story looks like on you, but what it feels like, and what a day in the life of that story would be like. Then come back and write down three or four new habits that you will do daily, weekly, or monthly which will get you to start living this story today. As you think about these habits, make sure they are measurable. Here are a few examples:

Goal (not easy to measure)	→	Habit (easy to measure)
Be healthier	→	Go to the gym 3 times a week
Save more money	→	Add $25 per paycheck to my savings account
Spend less time watching TV	→	Watch 2 hours (or less) of TV a day

Keep it to three or four because tackling too many new habits at once can be overwhelming and **then you give up**. Also, tackling too few habits will make it impossible to see how you are getting closer to your story, and **then you give up** (*see the theme here?*). So, stick to three or four to get some progress. Remember, in writing your story there will be many chances for revision, so don't feel like you need to change everything at once. What is important is what you can do **consistently**.

A few questions to get you started...

- What is that habit you have been "thinking about" starting for a while that lines up to your new story?
- When you think through what a day in the life of your new story would look like, what do you see yourself doing every day?
- What habits do you admire in others that line up with your story?
- With the bad habits you committed to stopping now gone, what new habits do you have space for?
- What is the one habit that would make you most proud of your progress?

In With the NEW...

Write a few habits that you will start doing daily/weekly/monthly/etc. to make your new story real:

Goal	New Habit	How Often?

"Successful people are simply those with successful habits." –Brian Tracy

Keeping an Eye on Your Habits

Something to think about...

Now that you have zeroed in on the new habits that will help bring your story to life, let's talk about how you will see if you are actually practicing them. Unfortunately, just asking yourself won't work because memory (*not just yours, but everyone's*) is unreliable. All people (*you included*) tend to flavor the answer with what they *would like to believe* about themselves. This either leads to giving more credit than is deserved or being a harsher judge than necessary. Here we just want to be accurate, for better or worse, so we can understand if the change is actually working (*Yeah!*) or if a revision is needed (*Aw! But that's ok too*).

Since we can't rely on your faulty memory, in this step you will think through (*and set up*) ways that you plan to track those new habits. This is your chance to be creative. You don't only want to track them, but you want to track them in a way that gets you excited to do it and stay consistent.

Some inspiration to get you started...

- Do a web search for "Habit Trackers," and you will get an abundance of ideas, everything from the simple to the beautifully artistic. Find a few that get you excited.

- Write a simple checklist of your new habits and keep it clearly visible (*think refrigerator, bathroom sink, above your desk, screen saver on your phone*) of your new habits. Physically check them off as you practice the habit.

- Re-live grade school and creatively decorate one index card for each habit. Then hang them somewhere you will see them often throughout the day.

- Get a journal specifically for writing down a few lines at the end of every day, and grade yourself on how you are doing against your new habits.

- Find someone to partner with on the goal/habit so you both can help keep each other on track.

Keeping an Eye on Your Habits

"A goal without a plan is just a wish." —Antoine de Saint-Exupéry

Get creative on how you will keep your new habits front and center, and how you can tell if you actually are doing them.

New Habit	How will you keep track if you did it or not?	Have you created the tracker?
		☐ yes
		☐ yes
		☐ yes
		☐ yes

Whose Life Is This Anyway?! Making Your Life Your Story

In Summary

Something to think about...

Now comes the time to begin to wrap up your new story with a lovely big bow. It's time to summarize your new story in such a neon-colored way that when you're tempted to slip back into old habits or need convincing why the effort will be worth it in the end, you have something short and sweet to help snap you back. Think of this as the shorthand representation of your new story.

Here's another opportunity to dial way up on your creativity. Choose two or three words, and pick a picture that summarizes your new story. For some people the picture comes first, and the words follow. Either way it's totally up to you.

These aren't just words that sound good or that you saw on a poster with someone in the background climbing a mountain. These are words that sum up all your dreams for what your new story is going to bring to you. It's important that you take the time to think carefully about these words. Roll them around in your mind until you pick the perfect words that, when said together, get you excited, thinking about your new story.

Word	→	**Picture**
Confidence	→	You, dressed as your favorite super hero
Joyful	→	Children laughing
Peaceful	→	Watching the sunset on a beach

A few questions to get you started...

- When you think of this new story of your life that you are writing, what feelings do you have?
- When you think of who you will be in this new life, pick one word to describe who that version of you is?
- When others meet you, what key words would you like them to use to describe you?
- When you think of this new story, what picture comes to mind?
- When you see yourself fully living this new story, what does that scene look like?

"Make your vision so clear that your fears become irrelevant."
—Unknown

words

1

2

3

& a picture

Feel free to draw it (stick figures welcome) or print out a picture and tape it below.

Making it Stick

Something to think about...

You made it! You're one single, tiny step away from no longer just *thinking* about your new story but actually *doing things* to make it a reality. Before we get to this final part, take some time for a dance break to celebrate the work you've already done! (I'll wait...)

Not only are you clearer about your story and what gets in your way, you have also wrestled the pen away from those real or imaginary situations that you felt were controlling your story. You now have taken the pen firmly in hand to write the story for yourself! Understanding this and doing something about it is a HUGE step.

This final piece just helps put some additional supports in place to help cheer you on as you practice living in your new story:

- **Keep it Visible** - Where will you keep your summary words/pictures so they can help keep your new story real for you?
- **A Helping Hand** - Who can help both by encouraging you and keeping you committed to your new habits?
- **Time to Party** - How will you celebrate when you've successfully practiced your new habit?
- **A Reminder That This Isn't Forever** - When is the next date you should give your story a re-look and start on the next revision?

A few questions to get you started...

- Where is a good place that you look every day that would be an ideal location to keep your Summary visible?
- Who in your circle of friends/family/co-workers/peers will cheer you on when you need it, and give you some tough love when you're not doing the things you committed to?
- What is something you can do for yourself as a pat on the back for the hard work you're doing creating new habits? When is a good time to celebrate the new habit?
- Every story needs revisions based on how quickly you can tell if your new habits are working or not. How soon do you think you should start on your next revision?

Making it Stick
Last Piece of the Puzzle...

Keep it Visible
Where will you keep your summary words/pictures so they can help keep your new story alive for you?

Time to Party
How will you celebrate when you have successfully practiced your new habit?

A Helping Hand
Who can help both by encouraging you and keeping you committed to your new habits?

A Reminder that this isn't Forever
When is the next date you should give your story a re-look and start on the next revision? Stop RIGHT NOW and put a reminder on your calendar & the next page.

"One day? Or day one. You decide."
—Unknown

CONGRATULATIONS

to YOU for picking up the pen, now go write an amazing story...

Next Revision Date: _____

How I am making My Life a Story I Love

How I am making My Life a Story I Love

How I am making My Life a Story I Love

How I am making My Life a Story I Love

How I am making My Life a Story I Love

How I am making My Life a Story I Love

Contact

Join in the fun on our website or social media to check out the additional resources we have to help you keep YourStory one that you love. Also, we would sincerely love to hear from you. Feel free to reach out if you have any questions, or to share how you are making YourLife-YourStory.

Follow Us on Instagram: @YourLife.YourStory

Visit Our Website: www.YourLife-YourStory.net

Email Us: info@YourLife-YourStory.net

Call/Text Us: 502-209-7623

Made in the USA
Lexington, KY
30 September 2019